World's Bird Collection: Adult Coloring Book Bird Collection Vol. I

Advanced Realistic Bird Coloring Book for Adults

Copyright © 2016

For resale and distribution information, please contact us via www.booboone.com

Common Raven

Common Canary

Common Cuckoo

Mallard Duck

Emu

Green Java Peacocks

Moa

Swan

Eastern Brown Pelican

Eagle

Albatross by Delarno

American Crow by Gennadiy Lukaynenko

American Robin by Yulia Znayduk

Baby Penguin

Atlantic Puffin by Lena London

Baltimore Oriole by Yulia Znayduk

Southern White-faced Owl by Lena London

Black-capped Chickadee by Lena London

Blue and Gold Macaw by Natalia Moskovkina

Blue Bird by Lena London

Blue Jay by Lena London

Brown Leghorn rooster by Lena London

Goose by Yulia Znayduk

Cockatoo by Lena London

Common Loon

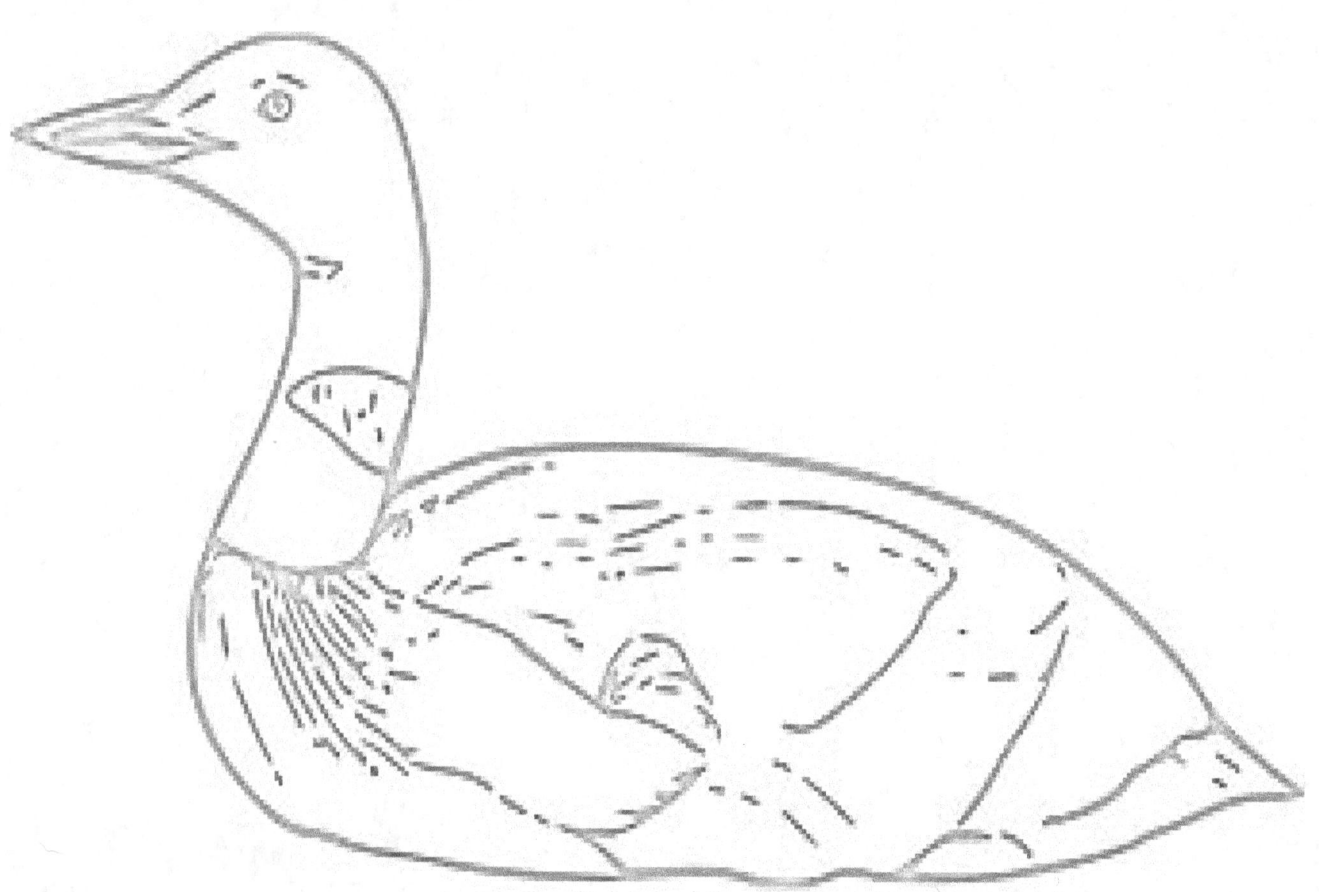

Common Nightingale by Lena london

Condor by Delarno

Crane

Dove by Loveandread

Falcon by Lena London

Flamingo

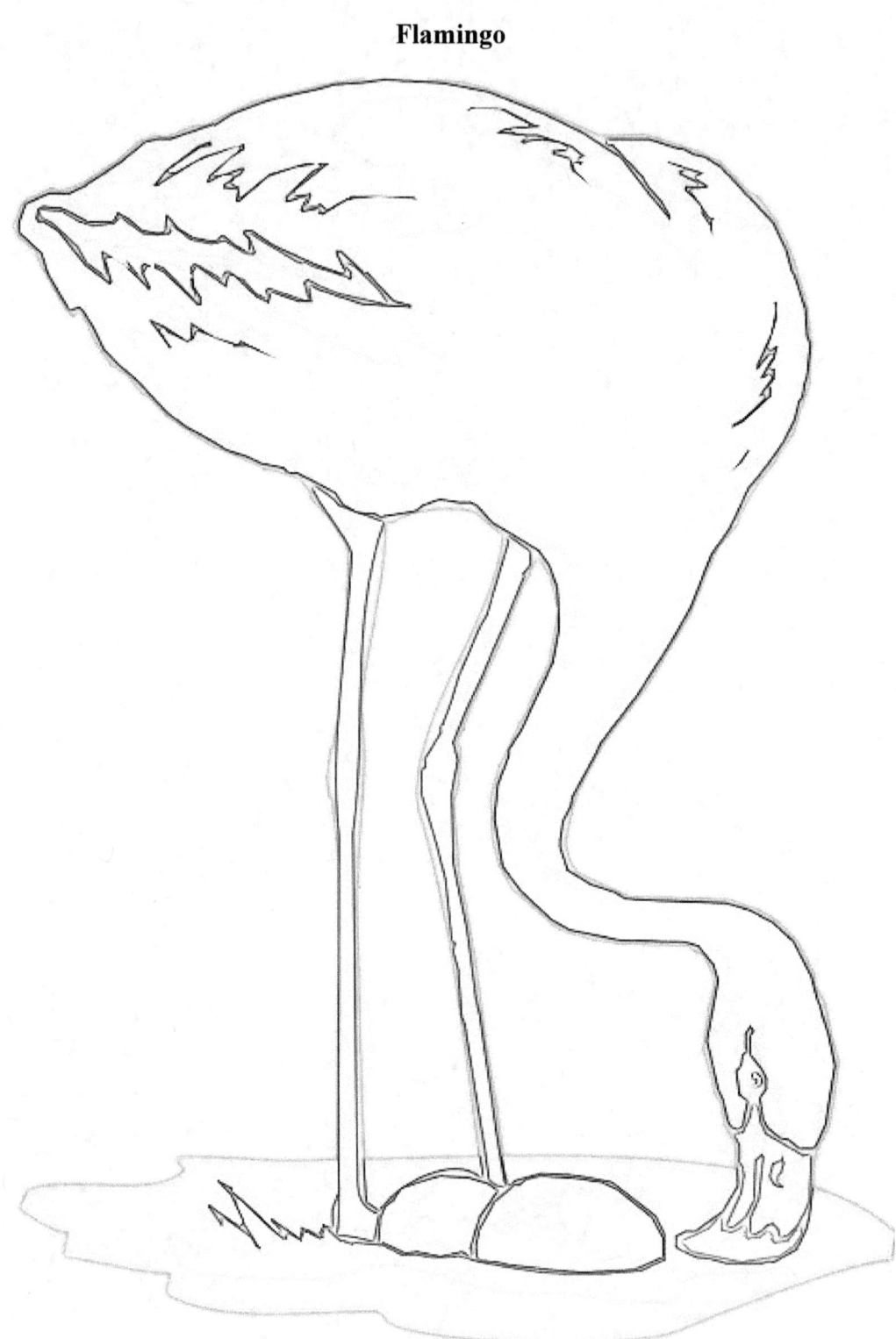

Flycatcher by Yulia Znayduk

Great Blue Heron by Lena London

Greater Roadrunner by Lena London

Grouse by Delarno

Hen by Artsashina

Hooded Crow by Lena London

Magpie

Goose by Delarno

Hummingbird

Bluebird by Delarno

Duck by Delarno

Keel-billed Toucan by Lena London

Kingfisher by Delarno

Kiwi Bird

Lark Bunting by Yulia Znayduk

Bat

Macaw by Delarno

www.ingramcontent.com/pod-product-compliance
Lightning Source LLC
Chambersburg PA
CBHW081226280526
45787CB00006B/2538